DOLLARS

&$ense

A Kid's Guide to Using—
Not Losing—
Money

Elaine Scott

Illustrated by David Clark

🖼 Charlesbridge

Published by Charlesbridge
85 Main Street
Watertown, MA 02472
(617) 926-0329
www.charlesbridge.com

Library of Congress Cataloging-in-Publication Data
Scott, Elaine, 1940–
   Dollars and sense: a kid's guide to using—not losing—money /
by Elaine Scott; illustrated by David Clark.
    pages cm
   Includes index.
   ISBN 978-1-58089-396-1 (reinforced for library use)
   ISBN 978-1-60734-540-4 (ebook)
   ISBN 978-1-60734-624-1 (ebook pdf)
1. Finance, Personal—United States. 2. Money—United States. I. Title.

HG179.S352 2015
332.02400973—dc23   2013022069

Printed in China
(hc) 10 9 8 7 6 5 4 3 2 1

Illustrations done in traditional and digital media
Display type set in Dirty Money by Estella Dawn Roberts and
   Chevalier by (URW)++ Design & Development
Text type set in Palatino by Apple Computer Inc.
Color separations by C & C Offset Printing Co. Ltd. in Shenzhen, Guangdong, China
Printed by C & C Offset Printing Co. Ltd. in Shenzhen, Guangdong, China
Production supervision by Brian G. Walker
Designed by Whitney Leader-Picone and Diane M. Earley

The biblical quotes on pages ix and 17 come from the New Revised Standard Version (NSRV).

For the bankers in my family—my brother,
George J. Watts III, and my daughter Cindy Scott.
With love and appreciation
                    —E. S.

TABLE OF CONTENTS

INTRODUCTION

read. Dough. Cabbage. Clams. These are just a few of the hundreds of slang terms that people use for money. Notice how much of this slang is based on food? That's probably not a coincidence. Food is necessary to sustain life, and so—in a way—is money.

In the classic film *Cabaret*, Liza Minnelli and Joel Grey sing a duet with these words: "Money makes the world go around, the world go around, the world go around." Yet a famous Bible quote says, "The love of money is a root of all kinds of evil" (I Timothy 6:10).

So which is it? Does money make the world go around? Or is the love of money the root of all evil? Surprisingly, both statements can be true.

A business cannot operate without money. Sometimes the owners provide the necessary funds, and at other times people invest, or put their money into, a business they think will be successful. Once established, most businesses hire people and pay them a salary. With the money they earn, these employees buy food, clothes, and perhaps a car or house. They go to the movies. They take a vacation. They give gifts to their children. They may be so busy working that they hire a teenager to mow their lawn or to babysit—even kids can make money!

Meanwhile, the businesses that sell the food, clothes, cars, and houses, or that run the movie theaters and the hotels at the

seashore—all of them are making money. So they hire more people, who in turn buy more goods and services. These are some of the ways in which money makes the world go around, which is another way of saying that money is needed to make an economy—the way a country uses and produces goods and services—work for everyone.

On the other hand, what people do with their money can hurt an entire economy, too. Greed—the desire for more and more of anything, especially money—can become a root of evil. Driven by greed, people have come up with schemes to cheat other people out of their money.

Enron was a giant energy company with headquarters in Houston, Texas. In February 2001, *Fortune* magazine named it "America's Most Innovative Company." Enron claimed to be earning more than one hundred billion dollars every year! That is one hundred thousand million dollars, and it's written like this: $100,000,000,000. That's a lot of money. People were eager to work at Enron and to invest their money in the company.

However, just a month later, in March 2001, *Fortune* magazine ran another article, titled "Is Enron Overpriced?" This article raised questions about the true value of the company. The truth was that Enron was not earning one hundred billion dollars a year. In fact, it was deeply in debt, owing more than thirteen billion dollars to creditors that had loaned it money. The fraud was gradually exposed during a two-month period, from October to November 2001. The company collapsed, and some of its executives went to jail. But average people, who had done nothing wrong, suffered, too. Those who had invested their money in Enron lost all of it. More than four thousand employees immediately lost their jobs. Arthur Andersen, a large company that provided accounting services for Enron, was forced to close its doors, causing another twenty-eight thousand people to lose their jobs. Without jobs, these people had no money; without money, they could not pay for food and housing. There were no toys for their children, no trips to the movies, and no dinners at restaurants. In other words, there was no money going back into the economy.

When the spending stops, everyone suffers. Some economists—people who study the economy—believe that the

Enron scandal helped bring about the economic decline known as the Great Recession (2007–2009), from which we are all still recovering.

That Bible verse, written around two thousand years ago, is often misquoted as "Money is the root of all evil." That isn't accurate; money itself is neutral, neither good nor bad. But money is important, because in many ways it does make the world go around, depending on how you use it. In 1931 car manufacturer Henry Ford said, "Money is like an arm or a leg—use it or lose it." The question is, how will you use it?

Many items, such as cars, televisions, games, and toys, come with instructions that explain how to operate the product. Unfortunately, money doesn't come with a set of instructions. Many people learn how to use it—or lose it—by trial and error. They make mistakes and learn from their mistakes. The information in this book is a little like basic operating instructions for money. After reading it, you will know more about money, how it came into existence, how it has been used through the centuries, and how it is saved, spent, and sometimes wasted. Once you understand money, you can make wise decisions about your own dollars and cents.

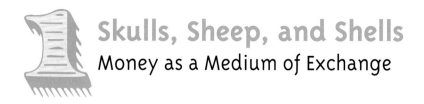

Skulls, Sheep, and Shells
Money as a Medium of Exchange

Have you ever traded one item for another? Perhaps a slice of your pizza for a friend's candy bar? Or maybe you've traded services with someone else: "I'll babysit your little sister tomorrow, if you'll feed my cat while I'm away." Exchanging goods (pizza for candy) or services (babysitting for feeding the cat) is a form of bartering, or trading. Bartering began long before there was such a thing as money, and it continues today.

Around 10,000 BCE to 4,000 BCE, our ancestors stopped wandering in search of food and began to settle down and live in small communities. Once they had established settlements, they learned how to domesticate, or tame, animals so they could raise herds of cattle and other livestock. Next they learned to grow their own grains and vegetables. People soon discovered they didn't have to do *everything* for themselves. Instead they could barter with each other. For example, someone who had a herd of goats but no seeds to plant could offer a trade: a young goat for several sacks of seeds. Someone else might offer to trade a basket of apples for a clay pot.

The barter system worked pretty well, as long as the person with the seeds wanted a goat, or the person with the pot wanted the apples. But suppose you had seeds, yet you didn't really want my goat? Or suppose I wanted the pot, but my apples weren't yet ripe? How could you trade the pot *now* for my apples that would be ripe *later*? The barter system failed to work at that stage, because the things that were traded simply didn't match up evenly. There was no common medium of exchange—no widely accepted item that could be used to pay for goods and services. In short, there was no money.

Once our ancestors came up with the concept of money, things worked better for everyone. A harvest of apples could rot, and clay pots could break. On the other hand, money—or currency—would not rot or break. In addition, it could be traded for something else of equal value. For example, the potter could sell his pots to the apple farmer now and be paid with money, which could be used to purchase apples later, when they were ripe. And if the apple harvest failed, the potter still had money to purchase food from someone else. In this way money, as a medium of exchange, helped the ancient world go around.

The first money came in many forms, and none of them looked anything like today's currency. In the earliest times, a medium of exchange could be a type of food, but it had to be something that lasted and wouldn't spoil, such as seeds. Whatever was used as currency had to be in demand year-round, too, so things like a measure of grain, a vat of wine, a portion of salt, or a precious metal, such as silver or gold, often served as mediums of exchange. Of course, dragging around vats of wine or bushels of barley was inconvenient, and gold and silver are heavy. What people needed was something that represented these valuable items but was easy to transport.

In 1200 BCE the Chinese began to use cowrie shells as money. They were portable, beautiful, and rare. Before long this medium of exchange spread throughout Asia and to Africa as well. Other cultures developed their own currencies.

Wampum—beads carved from shells—was the first currency used in North America. Developed by Native Americans, wampum remained a legal medium of exchange between Native Americans and New England colonists until the end of the seventeenth century.

Many Pacific Islanders had unique mediums of exchange. On the island of Yap, people once used stones as currency.

I'LL GIVE YOU TWO GOATS FOR THAT
Mediums of Exchange

Here is a small sampling of mediums of exchange used around the world from ancient times (before the common era, or BCE) to today.

Ancient Times

10000–4000 BCE: Livestock is the primary currency at this time.

1200 BCE: Cowrie shells become the earliest money used in China. They are brought to Africa in the thirteenth century CE and are still used in some parts of that continent into the mid-twentieth century.

1000 BCE: The Chinese begin to make metal coins in the shape of cowrie shells. Coins are made of common and inexpensive metals, such as tin or lead.

550 BCE: During the reign of King Croesus, the country of Lydia (modern-day western Turkey) produces coins made from pure gold and silver. Today the expression "rich as Croesus" refers to this ancient ruler.

118 BCE: China distributes the world's first folding money in the form of one-foot-square pieces of decorated white deerskin.

Common Era

I'LL GIVE YOU TWO GOATS FOR THAT

Mediums of Exchange *(continued)*

Common Era

806 CE: Once again China leads the world in currency creation by making paper money. Too much paper money is printed, however, and it loses its value. By 1455 paper currency has disappeared in China, and it doesn't reappear for hundreds of years. By the middle of the eighteenth century, paper money is once again common in China and Europe.

1791: Congress authorizes the creation of the First Bank of the United States.

1792: The Coinage Act of 1792 establishes the silver dollar as the first basic unit of currency in the United States. Originally, American coins ranged in value from a gold eagle worth ten dollars down to a copper half-cent. Today the US mints in Philadelphia and Denver make billions of new pennies, nickels, dimes, quarters, half-dollars, and dollar coins each year.

1816: Gold becomes the standard for currency in Great Britain. A paper banknote represents a specific amount of gold.

1900: The United States enacts the Gold Standard Act, making gold the standard for US currency.

1967: Automatic teller machines (ATMs) are introduced. Money becomes electronic, allowing machines, rather than people, to handle financial transactions.

1971: President Richard M. Nixon ends the trading of gold for dollars. The gold standard disappears.

Today: Paper money, coins, and checks are less prevalent as electronic banking grows in popularity.

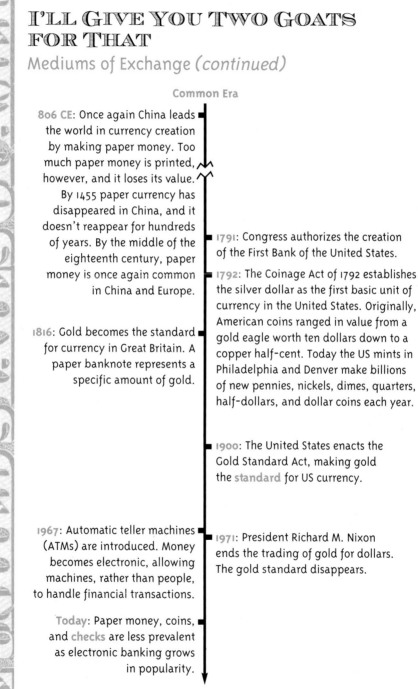

On New Hebrides (now Vanuatu), they used feathers. These are the heaviest and lightest currencies ever developed. The most disgusting currency ever has to be the human skull, which was used by the warrior headhunters of Borneo. Although they also used pigs and palm nuts as mediums of exchange, the warriors considered the skulls of their enemies so valuable that a skull became the standard for their currency.

A standard is something that other things are measured against. For example, inches are measured against a standard foot to show length. Twelve inches equals one foot, so we know immediately that something that measures six inches is shorter than a foot. It's the same with money. In Borneo it may have taken one hundred pigs or one thousand palm nuts to equal one human skull. Using the skull as a standard, it's easy to see that pigs were more valuable than palm nuts.

Fortunately, skulls did not become a common standard for currency around the world! Gold did. In other words, countries measured their currency against a standard amount of gold. They backed up that currency with actual gold, held somewhere in their treasuries. The United States adopted the gold standard in 1900. Each American dollar was now worth a set amount of gold, and gold was the only standard for redeeming paper currency. But how could the United States keep all that gold safe?

In 1937 the United States built an army post—complete with a vault—in Fort Knox, Kentucky. The nation's gold supply was shipped there on a nine-car train armed with machine guns on the roofs of the cars—and with soldiers who knew how to use them. Backed by such carefully guarded gold, American dollars seemed like a safe bet.

The delegates to Bretton Woods certainly seemed to think so. In 1944, toward the end of World War II, delegates from forty-four nations met in Bretton Woods, New Hampshire, to discuss how to regulate money exchanges between nations. The dollar replaced gold as the standard in the international financial market, where currencies are bought and sold. In turn, the United States agreed to fix the value of its dollar at a rate of $35 per ounce of gold. Theoretically, anyone holding a single US dollar anywhere in the world could exchange that dollar for its equivalent in gold.

But what if everyone in the world suddenly wanted to exchange their dollars for gold? There wasn't enough gold in Fort Knox to redeem them all. Fearing an economic disaster, President Richard M. Nixon announced on August 15, 1971, that the United States would no longer trade dollars for gold. The gold standard had come to an end.

Today the value of the American dollar and the currencies of other nations fluctuates—moves up and down—according to many factors. How much confidence people have in a country's government affects the value of its currency. To an extent, so does the price of an ounce of gold. But because the price of gold is no longer regulated, or set by law, its value is determined by supply and demand. If there's a lot of gold (a big supply) but not many people want to buy it (a low demand), then the price will go down. On the other hand, if there's a big demand and not much supply, then the price will go up.

YOU'VE GOT IT AND I WANT IT
The Law of Supply and Demand

Supply and demand is a basic rule of economics that states that the price of any resource, such as gold or oil or sugar, is determined by how much of the item is available (supply) and how many people want to buy it (demand). Usually, as demand for any item increases, the price for it rises.

But when the demand increases, others start to produce the same or similar items, increasing the supply, so the price drops. In the late 1970s, when a very simple home computer was new and rare, it cost thousands of dollars. Today you can purchase a powerful home computer in stores across the country for hundreds, not thousands, of dollars.

Computer prices fell because of competition, but prices can also fall due to little or no demand for a product. Few people want to buy last year's computer; however, if they do, the price will be a bargain.

When the demand for an item is equal to the supply of the item, an economist would say the price has reached equilibrium. In other words, the price is steady and probably fair.

NO MATTER WHAT YOU CALL IT, IT'S STILL MONEY
A Sampling of Today's Currencies

Here are just a few of the approximately 182 currencies circulating in the world at this moment:

Afghanistan: afghani

Angola: kwanza

Australia: Australian dollar

Bolivia: boliviano

Brazil: real

China: yuan renminbi

European Union: euro

Haiti: gourde

India: Indian rupee

Israel: new shekel

Japan: yen

Mexico: Mexican new peso

Russian Federation: Russian ruble

United States: American dollar

Currency operates in a similar manner. Economists talk about "strong" and "weak" currencies. As the name implies, a strong currency has more purchasing power than a currency that is considered weak. When the US dollar is strong compared to, say, the euro, it takes fewer dollars to purchase an equivalent amount of euros. With a strong dollar, you might be able to buy a single euro for about $1.30. But if the dollar is weak, then it might take as much as $1.60 to buy that same euro. Currency values fluctuate daily around the world.

Many countries still tie their currency to the US dollar. They have confidence in the basic economic systems of the United States—in the rules and regulations that govern its financial institutions, including banks. However, American banking regulations didn't happen overnight; they had their beginnings in the ancient world.

# Worry, Worry, Worry!
Keeping Money Safe

Where do you keep your money? In your pocket? In a piggy bank? In a real bank? Do you think your money is safe?

Money—whether it's in the form of bushels of grain or nuggets of gold—is a valuable resource, and anyone who has a valuable resource wants to keep it safe. Our ancestors were no different. There was always the danger that cattle would be stolen or grain would rot in the field, so they looked for safe places to keep these belongings. Though the ancients may not have called it that, what they needed was a bank.

Evidence of the earliest banks dates back to ancient Mesopotamia, an area between the Tigris and Euphrates Rivers that is often called "the cradle of civilization." Hammurabi

(c. 1810–1750 BCE) was the king who united all of Mesopotamia into the kingdom of Babylon. By the time of Hammurabi's reign, people were "depositing" their extra cattle, grain, vats of wine, and other precious resources in Babylon's temples and palaces. These were safe places, much more strongly built than the average person's dwelling and always staffed by many people. The priests of the temples and the noblemen of the palaces not only took in people's deposits; they also made loans. Borrowing resources and repaying loans were so important to the Babylonians that they set up rules and regulations regarding these transactions. Those rules are contained in the set of laws called the Code of Hammurabi.

In the millennia that followed Hammurabi's rule, the practice of depositing valuables in safe buildings spread from Mesopotamia into Egypt, India, China, Greece, and Rome. Then, in 476 CE, the Roman Empire fell. The chaotic period that followed is known as the Early Middle Ages (476–1000). Sometimes

"AN EYE FOR AN EYE"
The Code of Hammurabi

In ancient Babylon the Code of Hammurabi established 282 laws on a variety of subjects. In criminal cases the law attempted to make the punishment fit the crime. For example, if a man put out the eye of another man, one of his own eyes would be put out; if he knocked out another man's tooth, one of his own teeth would be knocked out. This view is often expressed today in the phrase "an eye for an eye and a tooth for a tooth."

One of the earliest known sets of laws, the code was chiseled into eight-foot-tall stone tablets called stelae, which were discovered in Persia (modern-day Iran) in 1901. The stelae are now on display at the Louvre Museum in Paris, France.

referred to as the Dark Ages, this was a period when European civilization did not move forward, but instead went backward. Ignorance and superstition took over people's lives. The rule of written law disappeared. For the most part, writing disappeared, and without writing there were no records. Without records, banking disappeared, too. People who had anything of value kept it on their person, or hid it from the thieves who roamed the land.

After several centuries of lawlessness, a period of discovery, invention, and conquest gradually emerged. During this period—the High Middle Ages (from the eleventh to the thirteenth century)—the Crusades took place. Christian warriors from Western

Europe marched toward Jerusalem, determined to take the Holy Land from the Muslims (people who practice Islam). The Muslims considered Jerusalem one of *their* holy cities. But by the end of the First Crusade (1096–1099), the Crusaders had taken control of the cities of Jerusalem, Edessa, Antioch, and Tripoli. When word of their conquest spread, thousands of Christians made the pilgrimage to Jerusalem to see the sites in the holy city.

Travel in the Middle Ages was full of danger. Bandits lurked everywhere. There were few safe places to rest for the night. Pilgrims were robbed, kidnapped, or slaughtered by roaming bands of thugs. In 1119, former Crusaders began an order—the Knights Templar—to protect pilgrims during their travels. To join the order, a man had to take a vow of poverty, chastity, and obedience. He also had to give all his wealth to the order, which grew richer and richer.

The Knights Templar set up communities in England and France, and along the pilgrimage route that led from Europe to

YOU CAN'T TAKE IT WITH YOU
Letters of Credit

Letters of credit provided pilgrims with a safe and easy way to travel and still have access to their wealth. A pilgrim in France could take all his valuables to the local community of Knights Templar in Paris. The knights would receive the valuables, calculate their worth, and issue a letter of credit to the pilgrim. The pilgrim could then depart on his pilgrimage, carrying little of value with him—just his letter of credit. As his journey continued, if he needed some money, he could stop at another Knights Templar community along the way, present his letter of credit, and get money. When he reached the Knights Templar headquarters in Jerusalem (or later, in Acre), he could collect any remaining credit in cash.

the Holy Land. Travelers could use a Knights Templar community as a kind of "rest and resupply" stop along the way to Jerusalem. By 1129 Pope Honorius II, the head of the Roman Catholic Church, had endorsed the Knights Templar. Any contributions made to the order were now protected by the church.

By 1150 the knights had begun to allow pilgrims to bring their valuables to Templar monasteries for safekeeping while they were traveling. And the Templars provided letters of credit—a forerunner of modern checks—to pilgrims as well. In some cases the Templars loaned money to the pilgrims and members of the aristocracy to meet their various needs. Thanks largely to the Templars, safe-deposit boxes, letters of credit, and loans are a part of modern banking practices today.

In 1187 the Crusaders were defeated in the Second Crusade. Control of the Holy Land reverted to the Muslims. With that defeat, the influence of the Knights Templar as a band of fighting Crusaders faded. However, their banking practices—issuing letters of credit and making loans—did not come to an end until 1307, when the French king, Philip IV, accused the knights of terrible crimes. Philip, who had borrowed vast amounts of money from the Templars, convinced Pope Clement V to take action against them. On Friday, October 13, 1307, the pope had scores of Knights Templar arrested and tortured, and ordered them to forfeit their wealth to the church. As a result, King Philip no longer had to repay his debt, the Templars' banking practices ended, and most of the money in Europe ended up in the hands of the pope, princes and kings, and a few extremely wealthy families.

During the Middle Ages, countries, cities, and towns issued their own coins. When a traveler arrived in town, one of the first stops was the money changer, who—for a fee—would exchange the traveler's money for local coins. The most famous banking family of the time, the Medicis, started off as money changers working from a table in an open marketplace of Florence, Italy. In 1397 Giovanni di Bicci de' Medici moved his major banking activities into a counting room inside his brand-new palace. Soon after, he expanded the family business by extending war loans to princes and trade loans to merchants.

Pope Boniface IX, who controlled the Catholic Church's wealth, became Medici's biggest and most profitable customer during this time. As its wealth increased, the Medici family was able to make more loans. Soon its financial services spread across Europe, as far north as London.

The Medici Bank, like any bank today, expected to make a profit on these loans. But it had a problem.

The Catholic Church made all the laws—civil and religious—for areas under the pope's rule, which included most of Europe. The church refused to allow anyone to charge money, or interest, for making a loan. It called all interest charges usury and said this practice was forbidden according to the Bible: "If you lend money to my people, to the poor among you, you shall not deal with them as a creditor; you shall not exact interest from them" (Exodus 22:25). People were supposed to loan money out of the goodness of their hearts, expecting nothing in return.

But the Medici family had a business to run. They, among others, were able to figure out a clever way around the pope's rule against usury. Because they had banks all over Europe, the Medicis could make a loan in one country's currency and then

TAKE IT TO THE BANK
Origin of the Word "Bank"

"Bank" comes from the Italian word *banco*, meaning a long bench on which money changers set up shop. The definition of "bank" that means "a place where money is kept" came into use during the seventeenth century.

accept repayment for that loan at another location, in another currency—which allowed them to charge a currency-exchange fee. Bankers could add interest to this exchange fee, and it would be hard for anyone to detect. Soon charging interest was an accepted practice, and anyone who borrowed money expected to pay it.

By the nineteenth century even the church had stopped forbidding interest payments. Today banks always charge interest on the money they lend; it is perfectly legal for them to do so.

Interest is considered the bank's reward for risking its money to make a loan. "Usury" is now a term that refers to any interest rate that is above the rate set by law.

Money brings power. As banking has evolved, so has the need for rules and regulations to control the power that banks have. In the Middle Ages those rules were decreed by the church. Today they are made by the government.

In many ways, the birth of the United States was also the birth of a new banking system with its own set of rules and regulations. And, as everyone knows, the birth of anything new—whether it is a banking system or a baby—requires labor. Hard work.

 **New Money for a New Nation**
America Builds a Banking System

In early America each colony's government issued its own paper money and set its own paper and coin exchange rates. There was no uniform currency, which of course made trade complicated, since money needed to be changed from colony to colony, and later, from state to state.

In 1783 the American Revolution ended, and the colonies won their independence from Great Britain. Six years later George Washington was elected president and set with the task of structuring and running the new nation. Washington chose Alexander Hamilton to be the nation's first secretary of the treasury.

Hamilton had an idea to fix the nation's financial problems and bring about economic stability. He urged Washington to allow the establishment of a national bank, to be headquartered

FINANCIAL GENIUS
Alexander Hamilton (1755–1804)

Alexander Hamilton was the only one of our nation's Founding Fathers who was an immigrant. He was born on Nevis, a British island in the Caribbean, and raised by his mother on St. Croix, a Caribbean island under Danish control at the time. By the age of twelve, Hamilton was an orphan and already working as a clerk in a counting house. Though he hadn't had the opportunity to get a formal education, his brilliance with numbers and sheer hard work eventually brought him to the attention of benefactors, who arranged for him to attend college in New York at age eighteen. After college he enlisted in the Continental Army, becoming an aide-de-camp to George Washington.

When the war ended, the new nation was bankrupt. Washington, as president, asked Hamilton to become the first secretary of the treasury. A new constitution was being written to replace the old Articles of Confederation. Remembering how General Washington had had difficulty convincing the thirteen colonies to send money to support the army, Hamilton urged the framers of the Constitution to establish a strong central government with the right to levy taxes across the states. Hamilton also recalled how Washington's army had had to import guns, ammunition, and even uniforms, so he suggested that the new economy be based on manufacturing as well as agriculture.

Thomas Jefferson—among others—disagreed with many of Hamilton's ideas. Jefferson envisioned a republic with an economy based on agriculture—tobacco, rice, and indigo. The power of this republic would come from its individual states, not from its central government. When Hamilton called for a national bank, Jefferson argued that the Constitution did not allow the federal government to charter such a bank.

Even though he often disagreed with Jefferson, in 1800 Hamilton supported Jefferson in his race against Aaron Burr for president of the United States. Years of animosity between Hamilton and Burr culminated when Hamilton made disparaging remarks about Burr at a dinner party. Burr challenged Hamilton to a duel on July 11, 1804. Hamilton was shot and died the following day.

in Philadelphia, Pennsylvania, with branches in different cities. To fund the bank, ten million dollars of initial capital would be raised: two million from the federal government and another eight million from private investors. This ten million dollars would be used for loans to start new businesses that would get the nation's economy moving. Washington liked Hamilton's idea, and in 1791 Congress voted to establish the Bank of the United States with a twenty-year charter, or establishment agreement.

Not everyone liked the idea of a national bank. Most of the nation's money—and the ability to offer loans to individuals and businesses—remained in the hands of a relatively small number of bankers. State bankers believed a national bank offered too much competition for smaller state banks to handle. And this soon after the Revolutionary War, a general concern remained that British investors had too much control over the bank. For these reasons, among others, when the charter of the Bank of the United States expired in 1811, it was not renewed.

The United States' problems with Great Britain were not over. The War of 1812, sometimes called the Second War of Independence, followed. Wars cost money, and with all of the banks operating under their own rules, raising money to finance the war was extremely difficult. The nation's economy suffered as a result. So by 1816 the Second Bank of the United States was chartered. It was similar to, though larger than, the Bank of the United States.

As with the first national bank, there were those who opposed the Second Bank of the United States. Among them was

Andrew Jackson, who was elected president in 1828. In 1829 Jackson began to speak out against the bank, arguing that too much power was in the hands of too few people and that the British had too much money invested in the bank. In 1833 Jackson pulled out all the government money from the national bank and redistributed it into various state banks of his choice. Without capital, the Second Bank of the United States was doomed, and in 1836 its charter was allowed to expire.

For decades following the closure of the Second Bank, there was no national bank in the United States, and state banks grew

up like weeds. Before long, the problems that the earliest state banks had encountered reoccured. New banks simply did not have enough capital to operate securely. The value of currency also varied from bank to bank; because each bank issued its own currency, a one-dollar bill at one bank was not necessarily worth a full dollar at another bank. Furthermore, in an effort to make a profit, the banks made risky loans that often were not repaid.

In 1863 the National Currency Act (later renamed the National Bank Act) established the Office of the Comptroller of the Currency (OCC), a federal office that exists to this day. The OCC chartered national banks. The currency issued by the national banks was uniform and more stable than the various currencies available at state banks. In addition, the banks had to follow strict rules regarding the amount of capital and reserves they had to keep on hand.

A stable bank must have enough cash in reserve to cover the money that the bank has in demand deposits, such as checking accounts. If you have a demand-deposit account, you can demand, or withdraw, your money at any time. In the past, if people unknowingly deposited their cash in an unstable bank, they might not have been able to get it back when they wanted it.

The National Currency Act was a good start on improving the nation's banking system, but there still would not be a single central banking system for another fifty years. It took a while for lawmakers to agree, but under President Woodrow Wilson a plan finally came together. Wilson understood that people still worried about so much money and power remaining in the

MANAGING THE NATION'S MONEY
The United States Develops a Banking System

1791: The Bank of the United States is chartered.

1811: Largely due to Thomas Jefferson's influence and opposition, the Bank of the United States' charter expires and is not renewed by Congress. The War of 1812 follows, and the country falls into economic chaos due to no regulation of banking and credit.

1816: After five years without a federal banking system, the Second Bank of the United States is chartered under President James Madison.

1828: Andrew Jackson is elected president. He opposes the central bank.

1836: The charter of the Second Bank of the United States is not renewed.

1863: The National Currency Act (later renamed the National Bank Act) establishes the Office of the Comptroller of the Currency, which issues national bank charters and supervises national banks. Although state currency is still being issued at this time, the National Bank Act creates a uniform national currency that is backed by government reserves.

1913: The Federal Reserve Act is signed into law by President Woodrow Wilson.

Federal Reserve Banks

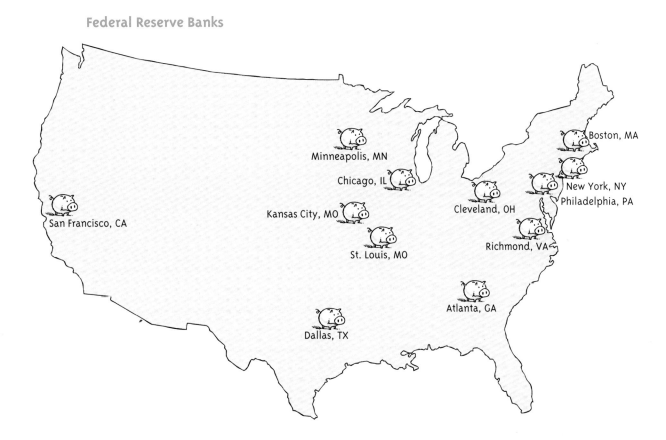

hands of just a few bankers. He addressed this by passing legislation that established the Federal Reserve System on December 23, 1913. The law called for twelve Federal Reserve Banks to be chartered in twelve different cities scattered across the country. The country was then divided into twelve Federal Reserve districts—one for each city.

The chair of the Federal Reserve System is appointed by the president of the United States and is then confirmed by the Senate. Member banks select the members of the board of governors. Federal Reserve Banks function differently than

KEEPING AN EYE ON THINGS
How Banks Are Supervised and Regulated

Being regulated means that a business must comply with certain rules. Banks that exist to take care of other people's money, and to make money for themselves, are called commercial banks. All of them accept deposits and make loans. In the United States, commercial banks are regulated and supervised by one of the following three government agencies.

The Federal Reserve System

Known as "the Fed" for short, this agency regulates banks within its twelve districts. The chair of the Federal Reserve often talks to the public and to Congress about the country's economic health. His or her words are taken seriously by investors around the world.

The Office of the Comptroller of the Currency (OCC)

An independent bureau of the Department of the Treasury, the OCC charters, regulates, and supervises all national banks, as well as federal savings associations. It also supervises the federal branches and agencies of foreign banks doing business in the United States.

Federal Deposit Insurance Corporation (FDIC)

This agency insures the money people deposit into their bank accounts, up to $250,000 for each account. The FDIC's bank examiners also visit banks to make certain they are following all the rules and regulations for sound banking practices, many of which are included in the Consumer Credit Protection Act, created in 1968. Banks that offer this protection display a sign that says, "Insured by the FDIC." Banks pay a premium, or fee, to the FDIC for this kind of insurance. The FDIC's insurance program is not funded by the federal government.

A bank's primary federal regulator could be the Fed, the OCC, or the FDIC. State-chartered banks are also subject to regulation by the state where the bank was chartered. For example, a state bank in California could be regulated by two agencies: the FDIC and the California Department of Financial Institutions. Each regulatory agency has the power to close a bank if the agency discovers poor management of the bank's assets.

commercial banks, which, like any business, exist to earn a profit. Federal Reserve Banks and the Federal Reserve System are a cooperative effort between private citizens—the officers of the banks—and the federal government. Together they form the central banking system of the United States.

Alexander Hamilton would be happy to know that after more than a century of political struggle, a national banking system was finally in place.

Money Comes In and Money Goes Out
How Banks Work

"Money" and "power" are two words that are often used together. In fact, many older banks look like the ancient seats of power—temples and palaces—with their imposing marble walls and ornate columns. Their appearance alone seems to say, "There's a lot of money inside these walls, and this building is a safe place for your money, too." Usually, that's true. There *is* a lot of money inside a bank, and it *is* safe. So how does that money get there?

All businesses have a product, and a bank's product is money, in one form or another. In the past some banks were privately owned, but today most banks are corporations, which means that investors provided some of the money needed to form the bank. The amount varies according to the size of the bank and to state and federal laws, but it can take more than a million dollars to start up a small bank.

So commercial banks begin with capital that has been raised from investors—but they still need more money to make money for their shareholders. A bank's board of directors may choose to raise more capital by selling additional shares of stock to the general public. Those who buy shares of stock in the bank become

GOING INTO BUSINESS
How to Create a Corporation

Imagine you have a successful pet-sitting business called Happy Paws. Since you are doing a good job of pet sitting, more and more people want your services. Your business is growing, and you could use some help. But hiring other people to work for you costs money, so you decide to incorporate Happy Paws in order to raise money.

You gather a group of investors—people who are willing to give you money in exchange for part ownership of Happy Paws. These investors now own shares in your business and are issued shares of stock to prove their ownership. They become your shareholders. The shareholders elect a board of directors. The board of directors then appoints officers for Happy Paws. Next, because forming a corporation is serious business, governed by state laws, you will have a lot of paperwork to fill out. Once that work is done, Happy Paws will be granted articles of incorporation (also known as a charter), and its name will now be Happy Paws, Inc.

Among other things, the articles describe the nature of the business, name members of the board of directors and officers of the company, and state how many shares of stock will initially be offered for sale. From the sale of that stock, you and your company now have the investors' money to use in order to grow the business. But while you may have been named president of Happy Paws, Inc., you are no longer the only boss. Now the board of directors has an interest in Happy Paws, Inc., too. If the board is unhappy with the way you are running the company, it could ask you to step down! In a corporation, the board of directors, along with the company's shareholders, have the ultimate decision-making power.

shareholders. The money raised from the original investors, and later from shareholders, forms the bank's capital—money it *owns*. But other people put money in banks in the form of deposits. For example, you may open a checking account or a savings account for Happy Paws, your pet-sitting business. The money you deposit is not the bank's capital; it is money the bank *owes* you, and the bank must be ready to give it back to you according to the agreement you signed when you deposited it.

Banks offer all kinds of accounts; checking accounts, savings accounts, and trust accounts are just a few. Banks also accept deposits from businesses, other corporations, and even governments. A bank deposit, whether it is large or small, is governed by the same rule: the money belongs to the depositor, not the bank. The amount of money in a bank account is referred to as the balance. People often talk about "balancing" their bank accounts, which means making sure they and the bank agree on the amount of money that is in the account.

Simple errors can occur when you are calculating your account balance, so it's important to work carefully. When you write a check, you should record the amount in your check register—sometimes called a bank book—and subtract it from the balance. Your check register is also the place to record any deposits of money that you add to your bank account. Any errors in subtraction or addition will make the balance you see in your register incorrect; it will not match the amount of money that is actually in your account at the bank. If your check register shows you have more money in your account than you actually have, the results can be expensive.

Suppose you need to get new supplies for Happy Paws. You calculated your bank-account balance to be $28, so you write a check for $20 to the pet food store. But what if you made a subtraction mistake in your check register? Perhaps you really have only $18 in your bank account and don't realize your mistake until after you write the check for $20. That's when a series of unpleasant things begins to happen.

When the check reaches your bank for payment, the bank will see that there isn't enough money in the Happy Paws account to cover it. The bank will then return the check, marked "insufficient funds," to the pet food store. The unhappy owner of the store will call Happy Paws and ask to speak to the person

ANATOMY OF A CHECKBOOK
Where Does the Money Go, and How Much Do I Have Left?

Checkbooks come with a check register. The purpose of the check register is to help you keep track of how much money is in your checking account. After you write a check or complete a transaction, immediately record it in your check register and calculate the total balance. Don't rely on your memory for this work. The more checks you write, the easier it is to forget the exact amounts. Any mistakes made in your check register are yours, and if you write a check for too much money and overdraw your account, the results will cost you money.

Each month the bank will prepare a statement of your account, which shows all the transactions you've made, any fees incurred or interest gained, and the money you have left in your account. It is important to balance, or reconcile, the bank's statement with your check register. They should match.

A checkbook needs to be guarded as carefully as any cash in your pocket. Blank checks can easily be forged, so checks should always be written in ink. Remember, the fact that you still have blank checks does NOT mean you still have money in the bank!

CHECK

Record the check number in the first
column of your check register.

NAME
Address
City, State, Zip Code

1234

Write the date here. →
_____
Date

Pay To The
Order Of   Put the payee's name here.
_____

Write the amount
of the check in
numerals here.

$ _____

_____
Spell out the amount of the check here.   Dollars

NAME OF BANK

For   You can note the reason for your check here.
_____   Sign, or endorse, the check.
                                        _____

⌐123456789⌐   ⌐000012345678⌐ ⌐1234⌐

The routing
number identifies
the particular
bank you use.

Your checking-account
number identifies your
specific account at
the bank.

This set of numbers
coincides with the
check number.

CHECK REGISTER

All checks are numbered—usually in
the upper right-hand corner. Record
the number of the check here.

Write the date of
the transaction.

Record the amount of the
check or withdrawal . . .
or the amount deposited
into the account.

Add or subtract
to get the
account balance.

NUMBER OR CODE	DATE	TRANSACTION DESCRIPTION	PAYMENT, FEE, WITHDRAWAL (−)		DEPOSIT, CREDIT (+)	$	
		Note the payee, or person to whom the check is written, or note that you deposited or withdrew money directly from your account.					

who wrote the check. The store owner will want you to bring $20 in cash, and then will give you back your check, which is considered "bad." On top of that, the store could charge an extra fee for the bad check—sometimes as much as $35. And on top of *that*, the bank will charge an insufficient-funds fee for the work the bank has to do to return the check to you. A bad check is often called a "bounced" check, because it bounces back and forth between the bank, the store, and the person who wrote it. A check written for $20, when you had only $18 left in your account, could wind up costing you a $35 insufficient-funds fee from the bank and a $35 returned-check fee from the merchant. Wow! That's $70 in fees for one $20 check. You can see why it's important to keep an eye on that bank balance and do your calculations carefully!

Most people are honest, and their mistakes are just that—mistakes. However, some people write checks while knowing

there is not enough money in their bank accounts to cover the amount. It is illegal to knowingly write an insufficient-funds check. People who regularly and intentionally write bad checks can be arrested, fined, and even sent to jail.

In addition to insufficient-funds fees, some banks charge a monthly or annual fee just for maintaining a checking account; the amount of the fee usually depends on how much money you keep in the account. The more money in your account, the less the fee will be. Banks also charge fees for keeping their customers' safe-deposit boxes in their vault, for handling money in trust accounts, and for other special services. If a bank issues credit cards, there is often an annual fee for the convenience and privilege of using a card. The bank also charges interest fees on any unpaid balance on the credit-card account. Interest payments are another big source of revenue, or income, for banks.

***

If you borrow money from a bank, it will *charge* you interest. If you lend the bank money (by depositing it into a savings account, for example), the bank will *pay* you interest. Since a bank wants to make money, though, it will charge more interest on money that it lends you than it will pay in interest on money that you deposit into your account.

Say you have $1,000 in a savings account at a local bank, and the bank is paying an annual interest rate of 2% on that money. At the end of the first year, you will have $1,020 in your account. You will have earned $20 in simple interest on your money. You can then choose to withdraw your $20 and spend it, but leave your original $1,000 in the bank for another year. In that case, it will earn an additional $20 in simple interest at the end of the second year, giving you a total of $40 earned on the money.

However, many banks and savings institutions offer **compound interest**, meaning they pay you interest not only on your **principal** (your original money) but also on the interest you have already earned—in this example, your $20. In other words, they pay you interest on your interest. But in order to earn compound interest, you must leave your money in the bank. For example, if the 2% interest on your savings account is compounded, then at the end of the first year, you will have $1,020, but by the end of the second year, the account will have grown to $1,040.40. At the end of the third year, it will reach $1,061.20, and so forth. Over time, compound interest can add up to a substantial amount.

It works the opposite way, too. If compound interest is being charged on a loan, then the interest a person pays on the loan can add up quickly. For example, suppose someone comes along and wants to borrow $1,000 from the bank. The bank has your $1,000 on deposit, so it has $1,000 to lend to the borrower. However, the bank charges the borrower 6% interest per year on the loan. So at the end of year the borrower must repay $1,060 on that $1,000 loan. The bank now has a **gross profit** of $60 on that one transaction—but of course the bank has paid you $20 for the use of your money for that year, so the bank's **net profit** on the loan is $40, minus the costs of servicing the loan

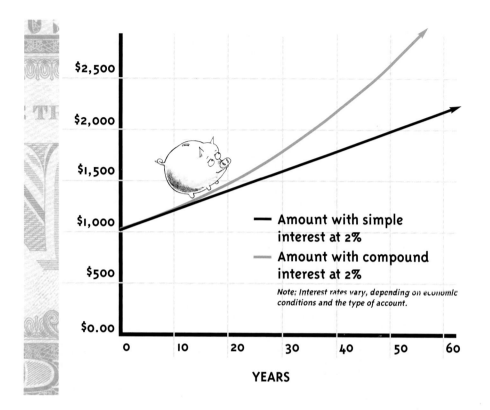

(reminding the borrower when a payment is due, keeping track of the borrower's balance, etc.).

Of course, most loans are repaid over a period of time. If it takes two years to repay the loan, the borrower will owe the bank $1,123.60, and if it takes three years, the borrower will owe $1,191.02. The longer the borrower takes to repay the loan, the more it costs in interest. The amounts in this example are small, but if you multiply these figures by trillions of dollars in loans across millions of transactions, then you can see how banks make money for their investors.

"But, wait!" you say. "That was my money they just lent out!" You're right—to an extent. Once deposited, your money

YOUR MONEY LIVES HERE
Types of Bank Accounts

Checking account

This is the most common form of bank account. A checking account is a demand-deposit account; the depositor can draw funds from the account on demand by writing drafts, or paper checks. With the advent of online banking, depositors can also pay bills directly from their checking account via computer. Banks may charge a fee for checking accounts.

Savings account

There are many different types of savings accounts, all of which pay some form of interest. Simple savings accounts, from which you can withdraw your money at any time, are demand-deposit accounts. They pay less interest than other types of savings accounts.

Money market deposit account (MMDA)

Unlike simple savings accounts, money market deposit accounts usually restrict withdrawals to only a few per month. Because these accounts typically earn a higher rate of interest than a simple savings account, the bank may require you to keep a minimum balance—money that stays in the account at all times.

Certificate of deposit (CD)

A certificate of deposit shows that you have agreed to put a specific amount of money in the bank for a specific amount of time (from as few as seven days up to a number of years). The bank, in turn, pays you interest on this money, because the bank knows exactly how long it will have the money to use to make other investments. A CD is a time-deposit account; once the time is up, the CD matures, and you may take your money out of the bank without a penalty. The interest rate on this kind of account varies from bank to bank, and it pays to shop around for the best offer.

Trust account

A trust account is often held by two parties, with one party (a parent, guardian, or employer, for instance) handling the money for the benefit of the other (a child, ward, or employee). For a fee, the bank will act as trustee, paying bills and offering other financial services. In the case of an estate trust, the bank handles financial affairs for someone who has died.

CREDIT UNIONS
You Own the Bank

Credit unions, which have existed in the United States since 1909, are another type of financial institution. They offer most of the same services as banks, such as checking and savings accounts, loans, and ATM services. While banks have "customers," credit unions have "members." People become members by opening an account.

The members own the credit union, which is a nonprofit organization. Any profits earned by the credit union are returned to its members. Most, but not all, credit union deposit accounts are insured up to $250,000 by the National Credit Union Administration, or NCUA.

doesn't stay in the bank in a bag with your name on it. The bank uses your money and the money of all its depositors in order to make loans and other kinds of investments. Even though banks are required by law to keep a specific reserve of money, either in the form of cash in their vaults or on deposit with their district Federal Reserve Bank, all banks lend out more money than they have on hand in cash. And yet, if you go to the bank and ask for your money, in most cases you'll get it right away. But it wasn't always that way.

Money Goes Away
The Great Depression

"Inflation." "Recession." "Depression." These are all economic terms that appear in the news every day. **Inflation** is any period of time when wages and the cost of goods and services go up, up, up. However, during periods of inflation, the value of a dollar goes down, down, down, as it takes more and more dollars to purchase something. Inflation can lead to a **recession**—a period of backward movement when spending begins to slow down and business is poor. For example, as the owner of Happy Paws, say you were paying $20 a bag for your pet food, and you charged for your services based on that food cost. But what if inflation hits, and the price of your pet food increases to $22 a bag? Now you are faced with a choice: either charge more for your pet-sitting service to cover the increased cost of your pet food, or see your profits go down. You decide to charge more for your services. Of course it's possible that your customers won't want to pay the higher price, so they don't hire Happy Paws anymore. With fewer customers, you have less profit and could even go out of business. This is how inflation can lead to a recession.

And if things get even worse, a recession can lead to a **depression**—the worst of economic times. During a depression, unemployment is very high and business almost comes to a complete stop. Severe inflation, among other factors, is what led to the Great Depression, one of the most desperate economic times in the history of the United States.

After World War I ended in 1919, things in the United States seemed to be looking up. The war was won, business was booming, and most people were confident the economy would continue to grow. As prices began to climb and inflation set in, people spent money on things today, because they felt that if they waited, the items would be even more expensive tomorrow.

During this period (1920–1929), known as the Roaring Twenties, **consumer confidence** was high. With great expectations for the future, people were making money and wanted to spend it to make more. To many of them, the **stock market** looked attractive, even though they really didn't know much about investing in it.

"Buy low and sell high" is a market cliché, but it describes a time-honored way of making money on the stock market: purchase something at one price, and sell it later at a higher price,

thereby making a profit. During the Roaring Twenties many people made money in the stock market by buying low and selling high. Tempted by this success, more and more people began investing in stocks. Why not buy one hundred shares of stock at $10 a share today and sell it in a few short months when the price rose to $15? That would make a tidy profit of $500 on the $1,000 it took to buy those initial shares of stock.

That's fine, as long as you had the $1,000 to invest in the first place. But many people didn't have it, so stockbrokers—

COMPANIES FOR SALE
Stocks and the Stock Market

As the name implies, a stock market is just that—a market where shares of stock are bought and sold. A share of stock is a share of ownership in a company. Individuals can buy shares of any company that offers its stock for sale on the stock market. If the company is successful and makes money, the value of its stock increases. Investors can choose to hold on to the stock, hoping it will continue to increase in value, or they can decide to sell it and take their profits. Of course, the opposite is true, too. A company that is losing money will see the value of its stock decrease. Investors then have to decide whether to sell the stock right away, before it loses even more value, or wait, hoping the company will turn around and begin to show a profit.

Of the eleven major stock exchanges in the United States, the two most notable ones are the New York Stock Exchange (NYSE), located on Wall Street in New York City, and NASDAQ, also located in New York City. Each exchange has different requirements for a company's stock to be listed.

Not all companies sell their stock on the stock market. Some companies are privately held, which means that their stock is owned by only a few investors. Facebook, for example, began as a privately held company, created by nineteen-year-old Mark Zuckerberg in 2004. Facebook remained private until May 18, 2012, when its shares of stock were offered to the public over the NASDAQ stock exchange.

people who buy and sell stocks and bonds for investors—allowed these customers to purchase stock on margin. Buying on margin means a person supplies a partial payment to a broker, who then loans the rest of the money needed to buy the stock. During that time, margins were often only 10% to 20% of the total purchase price. So if you wanted to invest $1,000 in stock, you had to come up with only $100, 10% of the total cost. You could owe the stockbroker the other $900, until you sold the stock or until you received a margin call, a demand for immediate payment. If a stock doubled in value, you could sell it for $2,000, pay off your margin account of $900, and have a tidy profit of $1,100, minus the initial $100 investment and the fees and interest charged by the stockbroker. During the Roaring Twenties individuals bought stocks on margin, and so did banks. And then the trouble began.

No one knows exactly why, but suddenly the price of stocks began to fall. There are many theories as to why this happened. Some historians say the price of stocks had been pushed up by speculation, as people made higher-risk investments in hopes

A MATTER OF TRUST
Buying Bonds

While stocks give an investor a portion of ownership in a company, bonds are a kind of loan an investor makes to whomever is issuing the bond. For example, a government bond may cost $100. When you buy the bond, you are making a loan of $100 to the government. Once the bond matures, the government will repay your money, plus interest. Bonds are generally considered safer investments than stocks. Governments—local and federal—issue bonds as a way to raise money, and so do corporations.

of making a higher profit. Certainly investors were speculating on stock in the country's utility companies—those that provided gas, electricity, and water to the nation's cities. In fact, in the 1920s utilities represented about 18% of the value of the stock market. Many utility stocks had been bought on margin.

In October 1929 things began to happen. Newspapers across the country reported that the government was about to institute a set of regulations for the utility companies—regulations that might affect their profits. Worried investors began to sell off utility stocks, leading to a massive dip in value. On October 23, 1929, the stock market lost 4.6% of its total value—and that was just the beginning of the losses.

The following day, October 24, 1929, is now known as Black Thursday. The day set a record for sales of stock. The average value of a share of stock in any company continued to fall. The following Tuesday, October 29, 1929, things got even worse. On Black Tuesday, prices on the American stock market fell 13%, effectively wiping out all the profits from the entire previous year. Alarmed, stockbrokers, who had begun making margin calls earlier in the month, stepped up the process. They went to their customers and demanded that they pay the money they still owed on the stock. Banks, which had invested their depositors' money, had also bought on margin. And they, too, were suddenly asked to pay up.

But what if someone didn't have the cash to pay a margin call? Then the broker could sell the stock at whatever price it was bringing on the market. Say you had purchased one hundred shares of $10 stock on margin ($1,000 total). If you paid only $100 out of your own pocket, you would owe $900 to the broker. If your stock then suddenly fell to $2 a share, your one hundred shares would now be worth only $200. But you would still owe the stockbroker $900! So where were you going to get that extra $700? Many investors—including banks—didn't know. They couldn't raise the cash to pay their margins. Most investors lost everything they had.

A share of stock represents a specific amount of money. As the value of those shares of stock fell, the money they represented disappeared, like dew evaporates from grass in the early morning sunlight—but with a lot more consequence! Thirty billion dollars was wiped out of the economy between November and December 1929. (In comparison, World War I cost the United States $32 billion in total.) By 1932 the market had lost 90% of its value. To make matters worse, as companies' stocks became worthless, the companies themselves went out of business and their employees lost their jobs.

It was a terrible time, and everyone was frightened, including those people who had put their money in the bank and had *never* invested in the stock market. As word spread that some banks had lost money by speculating in the stock market, frantic depositors lined up at bank doors, demanding their money back. Banks without adequate reserves—those that had lent out too much money—couldn't give depositors their money back. From 1929 to 1933, **runs** on the nation's banks caused more than nine thousand banks to close their doors forever. People who had money in those banks lost it all. Without money, people could not buy goods or services. That forced factories and other

businesses to close down. People lost jobs. Hungry people lined up in breadlines, waiting for free food. The Great Depression was in full swing, and something had to be done.

Franklin Delano Roosevelt was inaugurated president of the United States on March 4, 1933. The country was suffering from the effects of the Depression. People no longer trusted banks. The few banks still in business were in danger. If they were going to stay open, they needed a chance to retrieve some of their investments.

Less than forty-eight hours after he became president, Roosevelt did something drastic. He closed all the banks in the country for four days, stopping the runs—at least for a few days—and giving banks a chance to evaluate their financial situation. With the banks closed, there was not much money in circulation. People returned to ancient ways of doing business. In Salt Lake City, a man traded a pair of dress pants for a ticket on a trolley. A hotel in Oklahoma City agreed to let its customers settle their bills for anything the hotel could use in its coffee shop. One hotel guest brought in a pig! Pants and pigs became, for a time anyway, a medium of exchange.

On March 9, 1933, only five days after his inauguration, Roosevelt signed the Emergency Banking Act into law. Three days later he addressed the country through a radio broadcast called a "fireside chat." In a grave but calm voice, he said:

> *Some of our bankers had shown themselves either incompetent or dishonest in their handling of the people's funds. They had used the money entrusted to them in speculations and unwise loans. . . . It was the government's job to straighten out this situation and do it as quickly as possible—and the job is being performed. . . . We have provided the machinery to restore our financial system; it is up to you to support and make it work. . . . Together we cannot fail.*

The "machinery" to repair the economy included the Emergency Banking Act and the Banking Act of 1933, as well as government programs intended to address the nation's economic woes. These programs, called the New Deal, aimed to put people back to work and provide aid for those who could not work.

There were those who claimed that the New Deal interfered with free enterprise and capitalism. Free enterprise is the system that allows individuals to start and run their own businesses in a competitive manner with minimal government interference. It is closely tied to capitalism, the system that allows individual ownership of businesses, encourages competition in a free market, and encourages profit, all with little or no government interference.

There were others who applauded the government's actions. In support they pointed to the work of British economist John Maynard Keynes (pronounced *kaynz*). Keynes said that in times of severe economic crisis, such as the Great Depression, governments should try to create public substitutes for private investments, which is what President Roosevelt's New Deal did.

THE BANKING ACTS OF 1933
Saving America's Banks

March 9, 1933: The Emergency Banking Act legalized President Roosevelt's decision to declare a national bank holiday. It also permitted the Office of the Comptroller of the Currency to appoint an individual to take over any national bank that was on the verge of becoming insolvent, or unable to pay off its debts.

June 16, 1933: The Banking Act of 1933, also known as the Glass-Steagall Act, established the Federal Deposit Insurance Corporation (FDIC) and provided it with $289 million to insure individual bank accounts.

THINKING ABOUT MONEY
John Maynard Keynes (1883–1946)

John Maynard Keynes is often called the most brilliant economist of the twentieth century. During the Great Depression, he wrote a book called *The General Theory of Employment, Interest, and Money*. In it Keynes argued for government intervention. He believed that when an economy was growing too fast—a period known as inflation—the government should raise taxes to help slow the rate of spending. But during a slow or sluggish economy, when people weren't spending money, Keynes believed the government should reduce taxes and spend money on government programs. To stimulate investment the government could also lower interest rates to allow for easier borrowing. In more severe cases, such as a depression, he urged governments to take on debt in order to subsidize the poor and the unemployed. The United States took on debt to institute government programs that provided help for those affected by the Depression; however, in a departure from Keynes's ideas, Congress also decided to raise money by passing the Revenue Act of 1932, which collected more taxes from individuals and businesses. Keynesian economics are actively debated today.

The New Deal and its programs didn't work overnight. It took a long time for the country to come out of the Depression. The memory of those awful years stayed with everyone who lived through them. Eventually, however, companies started to hire again, putting money in workers' pockets, which they, in turn, used to buy the things they needed. Time passed, and the economy recovered. In the decades following the Great Depression, the United States moved through periods of inflation followed by periods of recession, and long periods of slow but steady growth. And then came December 2007—the beginning of what is now called the Great Recession.

A PRESIDENT'S IDEAS
The New Deal

Roosevelt's New Deal included the following economic programs:

The Civil Works Administration (CWA) created temporary construction jobs for the unemployed.

The Civilian Conservation Corps (CCC) paid a small salary and provided free room and board while workers maintained and restored the nation's forests, rivers and streams, and parks.

The Public Works Administration (PWA) allocated money for the construction of public works, such as the Grand Coulee Dam on the Columbia River in Washington State; the Lincoln Tunnel in New York City; and the Overseas Highway, which connects Key West, Florida, with the mainland.

The Works Progress Administration (WPA) provided work constructing or repairing highways, hospitals, schools, and airfields.

The Fair Labor Standards Act of 1938 established a maximum forty-hour work week, set a minimum wage, and banned most child labor in the United States.

The Social Security Act of 1935 is still in effect today, though it has been amended, or changed, over the years. The Social Security program taxes workers while they have a job and then provides a monthly pension to them after they retire. The program also offers aid to young children who have lost a parent and to those who are disabled and cannot work.

 **Money Shrinks**
The Great Recession

ost people can't tell the difference between a depression and a severe recession. Economists argue about the terms among themselves. In fact, there is an old joke among economists that goes, "A recession is when your neighbors lose their jobs; a depression is when you lose yours." The truth is, all economists agree that the Great Recession was almost as bad as the Great Depression of the 1930s. The Great Recession officially lasted from December 2007 until June 2009, but its effects lasted much longer. Businesses closed their doors. Stock prices fell. People lost their jobs and then their homes. Even as the stock market eventually recovered, many people were still out of work as businesses refused to hire new workers. Houses remained on the market, not selling, and their prices fell to record lows.

How did this happen again? Didn't we learn from the Great Depression? The answer is complicated, but a single theme seems to run through all of the various problems. There was simply too much debt in the economy, and it couldn't be repaid.

Just as the Great Depression was preceded by a period of inflation, so was the Great Recession. Prior to the Great Recession, real-estate speculation drove up house prices. People saw a chance to get in on a market where their initial investment would increase quickly. They borrowed money from willing and overeager lenders. Everyone—borrowers and lenders alike—behaved as if the values and prices of houses would never stop rising.

Sometimes people even bought houses that were more expensive than they could afford, with the idea that they would sell them in a short period of time and reap the profit from the increased value. This is called "flipping" a house.

Economists warned of a "real estate bubble." House prices had inflated in the same way that air inflates a soap bubble—fast. But like a soap bubble that is too full of air, the housing bubble was unstable. It burst. The prices, and subsequently the values, of houses came tumbling down.

Suddenly a large number of people owed more on their mortgages than their houses were now worth. If for some reason—a job loss, perhaps—a family could no longer afford to make their mortgage payments, they might try to sell their house. But if they owed $100,000 on the mortgage and they could only get $75,000 for their house, they had a problem. If they sold their house, they would still owe the bank the re-

maining $25,000 on the mortgage. Many people simply could not afford to sell their devalued houses, so they stopped paying their mortgages and moved out of their homes. Of course banks **foreclosed** on these properties, meaning they took possession of the houses. Across the country, the inventory of empty, fore-closed houses built up, but fewer and fewer people wanted to buy them. The law of supply and demand came into effect, causing the value of housing to fall even more.

Bad mortgage loans caused many banks to fail, fueling the downward spiral of the recession and the period that followed. From 2008 to mid-2011, almost four hundred banks failed in the United States. Fortunately, some banks were "saved" when they were acquired by other, stronger banks. And thanks to the government regulatory agencies established back in 1933, depositors in 2011 had their bank accounts insured for up to $250,000.

The housing bubble was just one of many factors that led to the Great Recession. Before the recession, people also speculated in **commodities** and **futures**. A commodity is a good that can be bought and sold and is interchangeable with other goods of the same type, such as a bushel of corn or a barrel of oil. As with stocks, people who invest in commodities hope to buy low and sell high.

Sometimes, in order to seal in a good price, investors will buy futures. As the name implies, a future is a promise to pay a specific price for a commodity at a specific date in the future. Futures work like this: In December you enter into a futures contract that says you will pay $100 for a barrel of oil on June 7. If oil is selling for $120 a barrel on June 7, then good for you, you've made a profit. You've bought your barrels for $100 each and can sell them on June 7 for $120 each. You have made $20 a barrel on your oil future. However, the reverse could just as easily happen. Oil could be selling for $80 a barrel on June 7. In that case, you've just lost $20 a barrel on your oil futures, because under your contract you must pay $100 for each one. Although fortunes can be made in futures, most investors agree that dealing in futures is one of the riskiest investments people can make.

Prior to the Great Recession, many people seemed willing to take lots of risks. As in the Roaring Twenties, confidence in the early 2000s was high.

In 2006 the price of a barrel of oil ranged from $50 to $90 a barrel. Oil climbed to $145.29 a barrel on July 4, 2008. But then what went up came down. From November 2008 to March 2009, the price of oil fell to $30 to $40 a barrel. Oil prices were down, housing prices were down, and the mood of the country was down as well. Many companies simply couldn't sell their products for enough money to stay in business. As a result they closed their doors, and people lost their jobs. Without a job, and many times without a home, people stopped spending money, which caused more businesses to close, and more people to be laid off from their jobs. By 2008 the Great Recession looked a lot like the Great Depression.

THE GOVERNMENT STEPS IN
Two Programs During the Great Recession

Troubled Asset Relief Program (TARP):
Signed into law on October 3, 2008, by President George W. Bush, TARP established a $700 billion fund to buy **troubled assets** from very large businesses that were in danger of bankruptcy. A troubled asset is anything—a car, a house, or even a company—that has lost some of its value

and is no longer worth what is owed on it. A house that has a mortgage of $100,000 but could sell for only $75,000 is an example of a troubled asset. Two of the United States' largest automobile manufacturers, General Motors (GM) and Chrysler, received money from the TARP fund, as did numerous banks, investment firms, and government agencies, including Fannie Mae and Freddie Mac, which had insured many mortgages for homes that went into foreclosure.

American Recovery and Reinvestment Act of 2009 (ARRA):
A stimulus package amounting to $787 billion was signed into law by President Barack Obama on February 17, 2009. The plan included tax incentives to encourage people to spend more money. It reduced some taxes on small businesses in the hope that those businesses would then hire more people, reducing unemployment. It also extended unemployment benefits to those who had no job.

NEW RULES TO GO BY
The Dodd-Frank Act

Many people believe the Great Recession was caused, at least in part, by financial institutions that had very little or no supervision. Rules and regulations existed, but seven different agencies were in charge of enforcing them, with no central agency in charge. As a result, there was a lot of confusion about what financial institutions could and could not do as they conducted their business. On July 21, 2010, President Barack Obama signed the Dodd-Frank Wall Street Reform and Consumer Protection Act. It contained major new regulations for the entire financial industry and established the Consumer Financial Protection Bureau, a new agency that helps consumers understand the costs, risks, and obligations that go with borrowing money.

Generally, people went from spending too much to spending too little. There was no equilibrium in the marketplace. Spending like Goldilocks—"just right"—was not happening. And without spending, an economy stops growing. Once again Keynesian economics came into play as the US government stepped in to institute large and controversial programs.

Some said these programs were good, because it was important for large companies to stay in business for the sake of the economy. But others disagreed, saying that bailing out failing companies provided an unfair safety net for them and lowered business standards across the country. The economy of the United States was in trouble, and there was no simple solution to the problem. Every family, every business—including the government—would have to take a hard look at its debt and make difficult decisions about how to spend its money in the future.

 **Can I Borrow Some Money?**
What to Do About Debt

In the first act of William Shakespeare's play *Hamlet*, a character named Polonius cautions his son, Laertes, about borrowing and lending money:

> *Neither a borrower nor a lender be;*
> *For loan oft loses both itself and friend,*
> *And borrowing dulls the edge of husbandry.*

The first line of this quote is the one that is famous—but the words that follow are full of good advice, too. Polonius is trying to warn his son that if he gets in the habit of borrowing money, he will lose the habit of saving it (thrift being one meaning of the word "husbandry"). Polonius is also warning Laertes that lending money to a friend is risky—he could lose both his money *and* his friend, especially if the money is never paid back.

That advice is more than four hundred years old, yet it remains valid today. For example, suppose you go shopping with a friend, and she sees something she'd like to have, but she doesn't have enough money to buy it. "Can you lend me five dollars?" she asks. "I'll pay you back." You lend her the money. The next time you see her, there is no offer to pay you back. You ask, and she says she's sorry, but she doesn't have the $5. How do you feel? As Shakespeare said, borrowing and lending between friends often isn't a good idea.

However, there are times when borrowing and lending money is important, even crucial. It would be impossible for most people to own a home if they didn't borrow money to pay for it. Without a loan many people could not afford a car. College tuition is expensive, and students often get a college loan to fund their education. In instances like these, borrowing money can be a good thing. The lender will make money from the interest charged on the loan, the borrower will be able to get the item right away, and the home builder, the car dealer, or the university will have money coming in to expand the business. Done responsibly, that kind of borrowing does make the world go around.

People borrow money from different sources. You may ask your parents to lend you $30. You promise to pay the money back as soon as you can. You are asking your parents for credit, which means you are asking for something now with the promise of repaying it later. If you repay that money in a timely manner, then your parents will probably be happy to lend you money again, because you have shown that you can be trusted. To use a financial term, you are creditworthy. But what if your

grandmother gives you $50 for your birthday and you spend that money at the mall, forgetting all about the $30 you still owe your parents? You may get a different answer the next time you want to borrow money, because your folks can't trust you to pay the money back when you promised. Trust is an important part of any financial transaction—whether it's between you and a family member or you and a bank.

Borrowing money from family or friends is usually a lot easier than borrowing money from a financial institution. For one thing, friends and family know you well, so they won't require a credit check. On the other hand, borrowing money from family or friends will not help you build a good **credit rating**, because most friends and family members do not report your payment history, or creditworthiness, to a **credit bureau**. Credit bureaus are businesses that issue credit ratings, or assessments of a person's ability to repay a loan. Your credit rating is one of the first things the bank will check when you apply for a loan.

Having a good credit rating is as valuable as having money in the bank. When you borrow money—whether through a credit card or a student loan—the institution lending the money, or the creditor, reports the loan to one or all three of the major credit bureaus. Every month, creditors report your repayment status to credit bureaus. Are the payments coming in on time? Are they a little late? Do you skip a month here and there? This information, along with your annual income, how long you've lived at your current residence, how many existing credit accounts you have, how many attempts you have made to get more credit, and other financial information are on record, and this affects your **credit score**, a numeric rating given by the credit bureau.

Credit scores are also affected by how much credit you have used, compared to how much credit is available to you. In other

CREDIT RATINGS
We Know Who You Are!

In the United States the three major credit bureaus are TransUnion, Experian, and Equifax. Each agency calculates a person's credit rating a bit differently, so it's a good idea to check your rating with all three agencies. A borrower's information is converted into numbers, which results in the individual's credit score. Scores range from a low of 300 (meaning it would be almost impossible to borrow any money) to a high of 850 (which means you are practically guaranteed to get the loan you want). You are allowed to see a free credit report from each credit bureau once a year—or if you are ever denied credit. Otherwise, for a small fee, you may order a copy of your credit report from any credit bureau at any time.

words, if you open up a credit card with a credit limit of $200 and you spend $175 of it, you only have $25 worth of credit left. That means you have spent more than 87% of the credit you have on that card. Even if you make the monthly payments on time, your credit score will go down, because the rating agencies don't like to see people use more than 80% of the credit that is available to them.

The length of time you have had credit counts toward your score, too. The longer you've had credit from different sources and have paid your bills on time, the better your credit score will be.

While creditors like to loan money to people with the highest credit scores, sometimes they will make a loan to someone whose score is in the middle range. But because the lender thinks the risk is slightly higher, the interest this borrower pays will be higher, too.

If you don't have a credit rating, it can be very hard to borrow money. But how can you get a credit rating if you can't borrow money? It sounds like an impossible situation, especially for young people, who are just beginning to manage their money on their own. Money you have borrowed and repaid to family members never gets reported to credit bureaus, so banks won't know if you've been responsible in those loans. You have to find a way to establish credit on your own.

Often, young people who want to establish their credit will open a secured credit card, one that is backed up by a deposit of money in the bank. For a small fee, the bank takes your money and issues you a card with that amount as a credit limit. A $200 deposit equals $200 worth of credit on the card. As long as your monthly charges do not exceed $200, you will be allowed to charge on the card.

Occasionally people need more time to repay what they have charged. Most banks set what they call a "minimum payment" on a credit-card balance. For example, a monthly minimum payment on charges up to $200 could be as little as $15, or even less. That sounds good, so you pay $15. But now you owe the bank $185—and have only $15 of usable credit on your card. On top of that, you have to pay interest on the remaining $185 balance—and interest rates on credit cards are among the highest rates there are.

"Interest? But it's my money that's behind the card in the first place," you may say. "The bank hasn't lent me anything!" That's true, but the bank has costs associated with the card:

SPENDING PLASTIC
Using Credit Cards

If you have a good credit rating, banks may offer you a credit card, even if you haven't asked for one! You might be flattered, but remember: credit cards make money for the banks or institutions that issue them. A bank usually charges an annual fee for its card whether you use it or not. Furthermore, if you charge items to your card and do not pay off the balance due at the end of the month, the bank will charge you compound interest on the unpaid amount. Banks also charge a fee to the merchants who accept payment with the card, which is why you may see signs in some stores offering a discount for those who pay with cash.

Used wisely, these small pieces of plastic with names like Visa, MasterCard, and American Express can be important financial tools. They allow people to manage their money and purchase things when they need them, which is convenient. But credit cards can be dangerous, too. Many people have used credit cards to buy things they want but do not need. Sometimes, they cannot afford these things, and then they are left with debt they cannot repay.

keeping track of your charges, sending you a monthly bill, reporting your payment history to the credit bureaus, etc. Charging interest is part of how banks earn money for their investors. On the other hand, you are earning something valuable, too—a good credit rating.

A young person looking to establish credit could also apply for a secured loan, or a loan backed up by collateral. For example, the collateral for a car loan would be the car itself. If a person didn't make the car payments, the bank would take the car and sell it for as much as it could to repay the loan. In the same way, the collateral for a home mortgage is the house itself. If the mortgage payments aren't made, then the bank can take the house and sell it. Sometimes a person will borrow money to start a new business. In that case the collateral for the loan could be stocks, bonds, or even the inventory of the company. Secured loans are preferred loans, and the interest rate on them is usually much lower than the rate on an unsecured loan or credit card.

Most credit cards are unsecured, which means that there is little the bank can do to get its money back if someone fails to make the payments. The bank can't repossess those things that you've already used, such as food and vacations—they're gone. As a result the interest rate a bank charges for an unsecured credit card is often quite high compared to the rate for a secured card.

Having and keeping a good credit rating is one of the most important things you can think about when spending your money. A good credit rating affects not only how much money you may be able to borrow in the future, but also whether or not a prospective employer will hire you for a job in the present.

A HOME OF YOUR OWN
Different Types of Real-Estate Loans

Most mortgages are paid back over a period of thirty years, though some people choose a fifteen-year mortgage. The shorter the length of the loan, the lower the interest rate will be and the higher the monthly payments. These basic mortgages are available to qualified homebuyers:

Conventional loans (no government backing)

Fixed-rate mortgage

As the name implies, the interest on a fixed-rate mortgage is fixed, meaning it will not change as the years go by. The mortgage payment also remains the same throughout the length of the loan.

Adjustable-rate mortgage (ARM)

The interest rate on an adjustable-rate mortgage is tied to current market conditions, so interest rates can vary. If interest rates go up, the interest on this type of mortgage can rise, too, making the payments increase. However, if interest rates go down, the interest on this loan can go down, and the payments will be reduced.

Government loans

FHA-insured loan

The Federal Housing Administration (FHA) does not provide the money for these mortgages, but it does insure them, so banks have less risk when making the loan. An FHA loan often has a lower interest rate and requires a lower down payment than more traditional mortgages, but borrowers pay a premium for government mortgage insurance.

VA loan

Another government-insured loan hails from the Veterans Administration (VA). A VA loan is offered to those who have served in various branches of the nation's military. These loans have little or no down payment.

USDA loan

The United States Department of Agriculture (USDA) makes loans for the purchase of family farms and ranches, as well as for livestock and their feed, seed for crops, and equipment.

I'LL BUY INTO IT
Accumulating Equity

Equity is a share of ownership in an object. If a home costs $150,000 and someone puts $30,000 down, that person has 20% ($30,000) equity in the house. As mortgage payments are made, equity in the house accumulates—slowly at first, and faster toward the end of the loan. When the mortgage is finally paid off, the owner has full equity in the house. The same principle applies when borrowing money to purchase a car or any other expensive item that requires financing.

Traditionally, banks and other institutions that lend money have used credit reports, combined with other factors, such as a person's income, to determine how much money they're willing to lend. For most people the mortgage on their home is the most money they will ever borrow in their entire life. In order to lend the thousands of dollars that it takes to buy even the most modest home, banks have strict rules. They will expect the borrower to have enough money—at least 20% of the value of the house (and maybe much more)—to use as a **down payment**, or money that is paid up front. So a house selling for $150,000 would require at least $30,000 as a down payment. That would leave the home buyer with a mortgage of $120,000 on the house.

In the past, mortgages were considered the safest loans of all. The events that led up to the Great Recession, such as banks lending to unqualified borrowers, changed that idea. But since then, banks have been working to follow much stricter rules about the loans they make, and are more financially responsible. Another way of being financially, or **fiscally**, responsible is to **budget** money, which is something that both individuals and governments need to do.

 **Where Did My Money Go?**
Sticking to a Budget

oney is a controversial topic. Everyone has an opinion on how his or her money should be handled—and how the government's money should be handled, too. In reality, handling money can be simple, because there are only two things you can do with it: spend it or save it. The trick—for people *and* for governments—is to learn how to spend and save money "just right." Of course, everyone has a different answer for what is "just right," but for all of us, handling money ought to begin with a budget.

A budget is a plan for how much money will be earned and spent during any period of time. Families, governments, and even young people with little money can set up a budget. A family's budget might cover the cost of housing, transportation, food, insurance, clothes, utilities (such as electricity, gas, and a phone or two), and savings—the categories can go on and on. Government budgets, of course, are much bigger, and young people's budgets are smaller. But no matter how much money is going to be spent, a budget can help anyone spend it wisely.

MONEY COMES IN AND MONEY GOES OUT
A Budget Worksheet

The figures in this worksheet are just examples. Your allowance or income could be more, or less. The important thing about creating a budget is that it allows you to keep track of your money and plan ahead for things you would like to do with it. You can create a weekly budget, or a monthly one—it's up to you. Work with a pencil, since figures can change. Perhaps you will be surprised by a generous gift from your grandmother! Your income, minus your expenses, will show you how much "extra" money you have. And if there isn't any "extra" money at the end of the week, or the month, your budget will show you where you spent it.

My Budget

Income		Expenses	
Allowance	$15.00 a week	Savings	$1.50
Extra jobs	$10.00 from babysitting	Gifts	$5.00
Gifts	$25.00 from Grandma	Treats	$10.00 for movie and candy
TOTAL	$50.00	TOTAL	$16.50
Difference: $50.00 – $16.50 = $33.50			

Some young people get an allowance every week. Depending on their agreement with their parents (and how much money they receive), they may be expected to pay for their own trips to the movies, snacks, music downloads, etc. Teenagers, who may receive a larger allowance than younger kids, might have to pay for their school supplies and even their clothing. However, some children don't get an allowance. Their parents pay for the things they need, and they may earn extra money for the things they want either by doing chores or by working outside the home. In the end, it doesn't matter how much money you earn or have; what matters is how you budget it.

Suppose you want a skateboard that costs $50. Your allowance is $15 a week, but your parents expect you to save a portion of that money and donate another portion of it. Obviously, you won't be able to buy that skateboard with your first week's pay. Assuming you save $1.50 of the money and donate another $1.50 of it, you've got only $12 left to spend. Then you have some decisions to make. How will you spend that $12? You may spend it all going shopping with your friends. That's fine. But then the skateboard will have to wait for a while. Or you may spend $10 to go to the movies, but save the remaining $2 toward your goal of buying the skateboard.

You can always speed things up by working for extra cash. It's important to learn the value of money, and there is no better way to appreciate a dollar than to work for it. If extra jobs aren't available, then you simply have to wait, saving up your money until you have enough to get that skateboard. Denying yourself something you want now, like a trip to the movies, in order to get something you want even more later, like a new skateboard, is another important lesson in learning how to manage your money.

It's not just individuals who need to budget money. Businesses and governments also need to plan their expenses. Politician Adlai Stevenson II once called politics the "people's business—the most important business there is." In a republic like the United States, citizens should make politics—the work of the government—their business and pay attention to it, because every single citizen is affected by how well or how poorly the government works and plans its budget.

A government has many responsibilities to its people. City, state, and federal governments all have to make decisions about how they will protect their citizens; pay for the education of their children; repair their roads, bridges, and tunnels; keep libraries open; and provide health services and other assistance for those who cannot afford them. The list goes on and on. All of these services are expensive, so of course a government needs money. It gets that money from taxing individuals and businesses on what they earn and on certain things that they buy. The government then creates a budget that distributes the income from taxes into various categories.

Problems arise when there isn't enough income to cover the expenses. Just like individuals, governments can find themselves in debt—so much in debt that it seems impossible to repay it. In July 2011 the US government was $14.2 trillion in debt, and it needed to borrow more money. How did it get so deep in the hole?

Before 1917 Congress had to approve every **debt issuance**, or sale of government bonds for the purpose of raising money. As the country began to make preparations to enter World War I, however, lawmakers passed the Second Liberty Bond Act to establish a **debt ceiling**, or debt limit, for the government. You could compare the debt ceiling to a person's spending limit on a credit card: the government could borrow up to the debt-ceiling limit without going to Congress for permission. In the years following World War I, the United States raised the debt ceiling more than seventy times, from $11.5 billion in 1917 to that whopping $14.2 trillion in the summer of 2011.

In July 2011 the government wanted to raise the debt ceiling again, this time by around $2 trillion, in order to avoid a government shutdown. It had happened before. In the shutdown of 1995, the government did not have enough money to keep all its agencies and departments running. Even the famous

THE NATIONAL DEBT
Whom Do We Owe?

The United States owes more than half of its national debt to its own citizens because individuals, organizations, the Federal Reserve, and state governments buy US treasury bonds as investments. Since the government promises to redeem, or buy back, its treasury bonds in the future, bonds become part of the national debt. In other words, the government owes that money. The rest of the national debt is held by foreign investors. Three countries—China, Japan, and the United Kingdom—hold most of it, with smaller amounts scattered among several other countries.

Smithsonian Institution in Washington, DC, closed its doors to the public until the crisis was resolved.

In 2011 another huge debate broke out between Republicans and Democrats, with the Republicans saying, "No, don't raise the debt ceiling," and the Democrats saying, "Yes, it has to be raised."

Those who didn't want to raise the debt ceiling said the country couldn't keep going into debt to pay its bills. They said they wanted the government to cut back on its spending instead. Those who wanted to raise the debt ceiling said we needed the money—not for new spending, but to pay the debts we already had. They compared the government's existing debt to charges already put on a credit card. The money was needed to pay the bill on the credit card, not to buy new things.

The deadline to raise the debt ceiling was August 2, 2011. If Congress did not raise the debt ceiling by that date, then for the first time in its entire history, the United States government would not be able to pay its bills. It would be in default. Most, but not all, members of Congress thought the consequences of not paying the bills would be as disastrous for the government as it is for individuals who don't pay their bills.

A government has a credit rating, just like a person does. Since 1941, the United States had had an AAA credit rating—the best there is. If the bills weren't paid, the country's credit rating would be lowered. That could lead to a domino effect: a lower credit rating would mean higher interest rates, not only on the government debt but also on the debt of everyone in the United States. Higher interest rates would cause everyone to have less money to spend.

And it wouldn't just affect the United States. Countries' economies are connected to each other. Economists joke that when one country sneezes, another country catches a cold. In this case, economists worried that America's "sneeze" would cause its dollar to fall in value. Because our dollars really do

GETTING DOWN TO BASICS
Major Parts of the Budget Control Act of 2011

The debt ceiling was raised by $900 billion. If the national debt increases to within $100 billion of the new limit, then the president can let Congress know that more funds are needed. Another $1.2 trillion is available when the president asks for it.

The congressional Joint Select Committee on Deficit Reduction, also called the Super Committee, was formed by the leaders of each house of Congress. The six Republicans and six Democrats on the Super Committee were in charge of coming up with $1.5 trillion in **deficit reduction**, or spending cuts, by November 23, 2011. Congress was given the task of passing the committee's plan by December 23, 2011, so that it could be enacted by January 15, 2012. Unfortunately, the committee was not able to agree on a plan, so the sequestration provision came into play.

THE HAMMER
Sequestration Provision

Since congressional committees are often slow to act, a provision of the Budget Control Act stated that if no plan was enacted into law by January 15, 2012, automatic cuts of $1.2 trillion would be made, half from defense and half from non-defense spending, during the period of time from 2013 to 2021. Since each party favored one or another of these programs, the threat of the hammer falling on all of them was seen as insurance that the Super Committee would do its job—but it failed to do it.

In January 2013, following the election of Barack Obama to a second term as president, members of Congress renewed their debate about whether sequestration would be necessary, and if so, what government programs and jobs would either be eliminated or reduced. Sequestration went into effect on March 1, 2013. The government had to reduce its spending by twenty-four billion dollars. With less money to spend, the government had to trim the budgets of the Defense Department, the FBI, and Homeland Security. Services to the public were reduced, too. Even the popular tours of the White House were cancelled to save money.

make the economic world go around, the effect would be felt everywhere, causing other countries to have financial problems. The stakes could not have been higher.

Finally, after months of heated argument, with just twelve hours to the deadline, a compromise of sorts was reached. On the afternoon of August 2, the Budget Control Act of 2011 made its way to the desk of President Barack Obama, and he signed it into law, raising the debt ceiling to a little more than $16 trillion.

Neither side got exactly what it wanted. Republicans, Democrats, and Independents will continue to debate as they struggle to find a way to handle the country's dollars—which are really the taxpayers' dollars—in a way that makes sense to us all. And all the arguing about how the government was going to spend its money took its toll. On August 5, 2011, Standard and Poor's, an agency that issues credit ratings, lowered the United States' AAA credit rating to AA+. It wasn't much of a drop, and many of the things people feared would happen didn't. But it was a warning. Just as in a family, the members of a government need to work together to control the budget and watch the amount of debt, while still paying the bills.

Conclusion
How to Be Rich Without Even Trying

No matter who is spending it—a government or an individual—money pays for necessities for us and, through charity, for others who have little or no money at all. Managed well, money brings us pleasure, allowing us to buy the things we want and need. Managed poorly, it brings debt that is difficult or impossible to repay, and all the miseries that come with debt. The trick is to learn how to handle your dollars so they make sense to you—and allow you to be a financially responsible individual.

Money does make the world go around, and you should use your own dollars sensibly. Still, people's worth is not connected to how much money they have. It is connected to what kind of person they are, how they treat others, and how they treat themselves. People with a lot of money who choose to keep it all for themselves, ignoring the needs of others, are poor in the areas that matter most—kindness and generosity. On the other hand, people who manage their money wisely and share what they have compassionately are rich, whether they have a lot of money or just a little.

Choose well and you'll be wealthy, no matter what.

GLOSSARY

adjustable-rate mortgage (ARM): a mortgage with an interest rate that is tied to market conditions.

articles of incorporation: documents issued by a state that create a corporation. *See also* charter.

balance: the amount of money in a bank account; or an amount owed, such as the amount owed on a credit card. The verb "to balance" means to account for money left in a bank account, after all withdrawals have been made. *See also* reconcile.

bank: a for-profit business that provides financial services for customers, including holding deposits in various types of accounts, allowing checks to be drawn on specific accounts, and lending money.

bank book: *see* check register.

barter: to trade by exchanging goods or services instead of using money.

bond: a certificate sold by a company or government guaranteeing that the purchaser will be repaid the purchase price of the bond, plus interest, by a specific future date.

budget: a plan for how much money will be earned and spent during a specific period of time. Also used as a verb, as in, "I'm budgeting my money."

capital: money or other resources owned by a business or an individual.

capitalism: an economic system in which the land, factories, and other resources used in making goods or delivering services are owned by individuals or investors and operated for profit in a competitive market.

charter: an official document that establishes a bank or corporation, describing the aims and principles of the institution. The verb "to charter" means to establish, as in, "My parents just chartered a tutoring company, Homework Help in a Hurry, and now it's open for business." *See also* articles of incorporation.

check: a financial document that is written to pay a person or institution a specific amount of money from a specified account.

check register: a checkbook ledger that allows the account holder to keep track of checks written, deposits, withdrawals, transfers, and bank balances.

checking account: an account that allows the account holder to write checks against funds that have been deposited in the financial institution.

collateral: an item, such as a house, pledged as security to ensure the repayment of a loan.

commercial bank: a bank that seeks to make a profit for its investors as it provides financial services to individual and commercial customers.

commodity: a good that can be bought and sold and is interchangeable with other goods of the same type.

compound interest: interest paid on both the original amount of money borrowed (the principal) and already accumulated interest.

consumer confidence: the attitude of consumers about their economic future. The more confident people feel about their future, the more they will spend. Less confidence in the future equals less spending.

corporation: a company owned by a group of people—its investors—who are represented by the corporation's board of directors.

credit: an amount of money available for a person to borrow with the promise that it will be repaid later, usually with interest.

credit bureau: an agency that collects debt and repayment information in order to issue credit reports on individuals. Also known as a credit-reporting agency.

credit card: a card issued by a bank or store that allows people to make purchases now and pay for them later, using a pre-approved line of credit.

credit limit: the maximum amount of credit available to a person.

credit rating: an overall assessment of a borrower's ability to repay a loan.

credit score: a numeric rating given by a credit bureau that reflects a person's creditworthiness.

credit union: a nonprofit financial institution owned by its members (account holders).

creditor: a person or business to whom money is owed.

creditworthy: qualified to borrow money based on one's history of repaying previous debts.

currency: money. There are many forms of currency in use today.

debt: money, goods, or services owed to another person or institution.

debt ceiling: the maximum amount of money that the Department of the Treasury can borrow to fund government operations. The debt limit is set by the US Congress.

debt issuance: the sale of bonds by a company or government for the purpose of raising money.

default: failure to repay a bill, loan, or other financial obligation.

deficit reduction: the process of reducing the amount of money owed, often by cutting spending.

demand deposit: money that is held in an account from which the account holder can demand, or withdraw, it at any time. Checking accounts and simple saving accounts are demand-deposit accounts.

deposit: money or other valuables that are placed in an account or a safe-deposit box of a financial institution. Also used as a verb, as in, "I deposited the money in the bank."

depression: a period of severe economic decline, usually marked by high unemployment.

down payment: money that is paid up front, before payments on a loan begin.

economics: the study of group patterns of saving and spending as well as the manufacture, distribution, and use of goods and services.

economist: a person who studies economics.

economy: the way a city, state, or country uses and produces goods and services.

equilibrium: the point at which the supply of an item meets the demand for it, allowing the price of the item to become stable.

equity: the share of ownership in an item, such as a house.

executive: A person who is in charge of managing and administering an entire company or agency.

Federal Reserve Bank: one of twelve regional banks responsible for maintaining reserves of currency, lending money to member banks, and supervising the member banks in their area.

fee: money charged for a service.

fiscal: financial; having to do with money matters. Also used as an adverb, as in, "the company was fiscally sound."

fixed-rate mortgage: a mortgage that does not change during the entire length of the loan.

fluctuate: to rise and fall.

foreclose: to take possession of collateral that was used to secure a loan, now defaulted.

free enterprise: the ability of businesses to operate for profit with little or no government regulation.

future: a promise to pay a specific price for a commodity at a specific date in the future.

gold standard: a monetary system that links the value of its currency to a fixed amount of gold.

gross profit: amount of money earned from sales of any kind, minus any costs that are directly related to making those sales.

housing bubble: a fast and unstable increase in the price of houses, usually fueled by speculation.

inflation: a period of time when wages and prices steadily increase.

insolvent: unable to pay bills or other debts.

interest: money that a financial institution charges its customers for borrowing money, or pays to its depositors for using their money.

invest: to put money into a business in hopes of earning a profit.

investor: a person who invests money in a business.

letter of credit: a document that guarantees payment for goods or services from a buyer to a seller.

loan: an arrangement in which a lender gives money to a borrower, and the borrower agrees to repay the money, along with interest, at some future point in time.

margin: money borrowed by an investor from a broker to purchase stocks. Usually the investor needs to provide a certain percentage of the margin up front.

margin call: a demand that all money borrowed on margin be repaid immediately.

mature: to become due, as in, "My treasury bond has matured, and now I am going to collect my money."

medium of exchange: anything used as payment in exchange for goods and services.

money changer: someone who converts, or changes, the currency of one country, city, or town into that of another.

mortgage: a loan used to finance the purchase of a house or other real estate.

net profit: a company's total profits minus its total expenses. In slang it is often referred to as "the bottom line."

on margin: buying stocks with money borrowed from the stock brokerage firm that is selling the stock.

overdraw: to take out more money than is in a bank account.

payee: the person or company to whom a check is written.

precious metal: a durable rare metal that has a high value, such as platinum, gold, or silver.

principal: the original amount of money borrowed, or the original amount of money deposited.

profit: financial gain; the amount of money gained after all expenses have been subtracted.

recession: a period of declining economic activity.

reconcile: to compare figures in a checkbook with those in a bank statement to make sure they are the same. *See also* balance.

reserves: the amount of cash a bank or other financial institution is required by law to have on hand at all times.

revenue: money or income from different sources.

routing number: the nine-digit code found on checks that identifies the bank or other financial institution where the account is located. Also known as the routing transit number.

run on a bank: sudden withdrawals of deposits by customers who fear that a bank may have to go out of business.

savings account: an account that pays interest.

secured: backed up by something of value, like money, a car, or a house.

share of stock: a unit of ownership in a corporation that represents a claim on the organization's assets and earnings.

shareholder: someone who owns shares of stock in a business.

simple interest: interest paid only on the original amount of money borrowed (the principal), and not on any accumulated interest.

speculation: investing in something that could be risky, with the hope of making a quick, large profit when the item is sold.

standard: a guide or model against which other things are measured.

stock: the value of a corporation's assets and earnings.

stock market: an institution where shares of stock in companies are bought and sold.

stockbroker: someone who buys and sells stocks for an investor.

supply and demand: an economic theory that states that when supply exceeds demand, the price of an item falls, and when supply cannot meet the demand, the price rises.

tax: a government charge, usually a percentage of value, against a person's property (such as a real-estate tax) or purchase activity (such as a sales tax). Tax money is used to support the government.

time deposit: money which must be left on deposit for a specific period of time before it can be withdrawn. CDs are time-deposit accounts.

troubled asset: items that are no longer worth the amount of money the bank loaned to purchase them. When the housing bubble burst, many homes became troubled assets as homeowners could not, or would not, make their mortgage payments.

trust account: an account in which a person or institution manages money on behalf of someone else.

unsecured: not backed up by money in the bank or by collateral.

usury: excessive interest charges above those allowed by law. The term was first used by the Catholic Church to refer to any and all interest charges, which were banned by religious law.

wampum: beads, made from polished shells, that were used by some Native Americans as a medium of exchange until the end of the seventeenth century.

RESOURCES

FOR FURTHER READING

Chatzky, Jean. *Not Your Parents' Money Book: Making, Saving, and Spending Your Own Money*. New York: Simon and Schuster Books for Young Readers, 2010.

Furgang, Kathy. *Everything Money: A Wealth of Facts, Photos, and Fun!* Washington, DC: National Geographic Children's Books, 2013.

Harmon, Hollis Page. *Money Sense for Kids*. 2nd ed. Hauppauge, NY: Barron's Educational Series, 2004.

Jenkins, Martin. *The History of Money: From Bartering to Banking*. Somerville, MA: Candlewick, 2014.

Karlitz, Gail, and Debbie Honig. New York, NY. *Growing Money: A Complete Investing Guide for Kids*. New York: Price Stern Sloan, 2010.

Sember, Brette McWhorter. *The Everything Kids' Money Book: Earn It, Save It, and Watch It Grow!* 2nd ed. Avon, MA: Adams Media, 2008.

Toren, Adam, and Matthew Toren. *Kidpreneurs: Young Entrepreneurs with Big Ideas!* Phoenix, AZ: Business Plus Media Group, 2009.

Vermond, Kira. *The Secret Life of Money: A Kid's Guide to Cash*. Toronto, Canada: Owlkids Books, 2012.

WEBSITES OF INTEREST

The websites listed below were current at the time of publication. To find out more about managing your money, try searching for "money and finance for kids" using your favorite search engine.

www.bizkids.com

This is the online version of the popular PBS show *Biz Kids*. Learn all about building a business through games and other resources.

www.pbskids.org/itsmylife/money

A site for kids about making, managing, and spending money.

www.usmint.gov/kids

Cartoons, puzzles, games, art, screen savers, tips for coin collecting, and more are all part of this site, which is packed with money information for kids.

www.themint.org

Developed by Northwestern Mutual and the National Council on Economic Education, this site provides information about money management for kids and teens.

www.richkidsmartkid.com

Play a series of games to learn more about money management.

www.kidsmoney.org

Financial resources for kids, teens, and their parents.

www.kids.usa.gov/money

Official government website for kids. Watch videos, play games, and even design your own currency.

Index